Venom.

Other Books by Abby Rosmarin:

In the Event the Flower Girl Explodes
No One Reads Poetry: A Collection of Poems
Chick Lit & Other Formulas for Life
I'm Just Here for the Free Scrutiny

Venom

a collection of poems

Abby Rosmarin

For a universe that continues to get what it wants,
and for those who know better than to get in its way.

Forgiveness (Part 1)

It was just a request — not even
that, but a question

one that no one else but
herself posed to
herself, and with it
an unearthing occurred, a cataclysmic
toppling down of what had been
built up, an eruption when the land
had just settled down, all because her mind
decided to ask:

"Can you find it in your heart to forgive?"

Don't Be Afraid

"I'm scared," she
said.

"Don't be," he
said – as he proceeded
to confirm
her every fear

Venom (Part 1)

Is there any venom more potent
than what remains after
all the optimism
has been burned out?

The Difference

The difference
between walking
away and
taking a step
back
is whether or
not I can see you
turn your back
on me

Scorned

They say hell hath no fury
like a woman scorned, but I say
the words are wrong – for
it's not the fire, but the
chill of a woman wronged

There is no more menacing a force to lay
in wait like a woman whose heart
laid open and bleeding for far too long
and for all the wrong reasons, only to learn
her only shot at survival rests
in sealing the wounds in ice
and avenging the things she mourns

Loyalty Lost

Sometimes
the lengths of a woman's loyalty
can only be measured by
how far it snaps in
the opposite direction
once betrayed

Chips

She points
to the brand
of potato chips on the counter.

"You know
your father – he preferred
a different brand," she says,
"but these – these
are okay, too."

"What brand do *you* prefer?" I say,
her words ringing
like the lady I met
who didn't
know
her favorite color – who never
gave thought
to her life outside
her addict

"Your father preferred the other brand,"
is all she can say
as if stumped, repeating
her previous statement.

"You can have your own
favorite
potato chip,"
I say

She is silent.

"Your father preferred those."

Fall For

It's the wording
I find interesting.

That we can fall for
trickery, fall for
scams, fall for
manipulation and
lies

And also fall for people.

Like every act is
something we would've
avoided had we
had a more keen eye
for deception.

Like every act is akin
to tripping on the hidden raised ledge
and skinning our knees
on concrete streets

Trusting Heart

My darling,
please be careful
with that giving,
trusting
heart

The man who seems
straight out of
a romantic movie is
most likely
reading lines
from a script

Tailgater

He rides up
on my tail
his car inches
from mine

and no matter how much
I speed up
he's aggressively
behind

In a break, I move
over to the right
to let him
pass

but instead of
zooming through, I like I
expect him to

He falls back.

I have not changed speeds
but now
I'm yards ahead

And that's when I see
it was never about the
speed

It was about someone in
his way – someone he could
close in on, while
that person blazed ahead
safely leading the way
through it all

Anchor

I said,
"I need something to
anchor me." – He said,
"What is an anchor, but
something that forces the boat
to one place
as the waves thrash it
back and forth?"

Funeral Home

I cannot stand the smell
of funeral homes – it smells like
all the wrong kinds
of preservation – it smells like
pretending death isn't
in every molecule in the air, ever fiber
of the tapestry, every petal
in the bouquets

It smells of the type of perfume
that follows you home – invading your
living room, haunting
your bed

It is the smell of honoring the dead
in all the wrong ways

Forgiveness (Part 2)

Forgiveness
before its time
feels like getting wounded
all over again

Bug

The other day
a bug
landed on my skin

I killed it before
I even knew what it was

How sad a state
to be
to act so ruthlessly
on instinct – to decide
without thought
to strike first, to
kill before
I'm bitten
again

Torment

The torment it must be
to be so desperate
to be heard
and yet to hate
the sound
of your own voice

Hell

And that is when I learned
"Abandon all hope, ye
who enter," was not
a threat, but
a safeguard, advice, a way
to cope, a reminder that
in this environment, giving up hope
would be the most freeing thing to do

For what is hell but persistent
hope, only to watch it
be dashed and reborn and
dashed again

We Both Want the Same Things

All I wanted
all I ever
wanted
was to make you happy

Little did I know
it was
exactly
all you wanted
too

Weight

Broken promises
cheapen words – until
they've lost all value
and there's not enough
glue
in all the world
to add back weight
to the things you say

Fake Strength

Anger is fake strength. It is
the chihuahua barking and
nipping wildly because
that's all he has to defend
himself

Aggression is just fear
trying to protect itself
using projections and
glamours and praying
no one sees the chink
in the armor

Narratives

I constructed brilliant
narratives
until time eroded the shine
and I was left with the dull
reality – the shell of a man
in desolate lands

the shining armor, just rusted
parts, the narratives all
falsehoods and
dreams
dead in the
light of day, in the
face of the truth

and no fairytale could
glossy it up

Forgiveness (Part 3)

Forced
forgiveness
is just
performance art

Flags

He waved his flags manically, his voice
crying out, "Go Trump!" the lines
on his face deep, the muscles pained
and pinched, as if on the verge
of hysterics, as if
this was his last shot before all
would be lost

Phoenix (Part 1)

"Remember
the Phoenix,"
I say – as I watch
my heart go up in flames

Direction

He pushes the baby
carriage with one hand and in the other
is a paper bag, a cigarette
dangling
from his mouth

Ahead, the woman talks on
her phone and pauses just
long enough to make sure
they're keeping
up

And from my spot at the red light, my heart
hurts
for the child in the seat, and
the direction
his parents
are pushing him
towards

Motherhood

May all mothers raise their
children so that
they spend
their adults lives
learning who they are, decoding
the world around them, and seeing
exactly where they fit in the
grand scheme of things

Instead of spending it
trying to undo
all the damage done, decoding
the toxic messages of
their youth, creating
distance
between the past
and who they want to be

despite their upbringing

Hotel Lobby

Two women cross the lobby, going
in two separate paths – one
down the hall and the other
across

One strides down the hall, her
shoulders back, head high, the click
of her shoes audible through
the chatter and the phones and the
busyness of morning

The other zips by, the way a mouse
scurries on, her shoulders
round, her head forward and slightly
ducked down, as if protecting herself
as she runs
for cover

The women make their way across
to where they need to go, their paths never
really crossing, but the energy they
emit ripples out, like two vastly different
boats, on two completely separate courses

Their waves only converging after
both are long gone

Callouses

Sometimes I sit back and
ask, "At what cost?
What did I have to
close off in order
to be okay
with all this? What had
to die
in order to keep moving forward?"

Mourn

What they don't get
is that I do not mourn his
death, but rather
the version of himself
who never got to live

Fuel

Anger might burn
a little too bright
and a little too hot
but at least it can fuel

Forgiveness doesn't fill the tank
or push the car
forward

Forgiveness (Part 4)

It's not on me
to find forgiveness
as if making it out
alive were not enough – now I must
search within and pull out
this piece for someone else

No.

It is only on me to focus forward and
fill my soul of all the
things taken and given
away – and give forgiveness only
to myself until
there is surplus to spare

Spine

How easy it becomes -- to
bend over backwards, when
you don't have a spine
to stop you

Chasing Skirts

How much it hurts me
to watch husbands
chase skirts
and the wives focus
their fury on
the fabric, the hemline, the
legs underneath, or
attempt
to shorten their own skirts
as a way to win the husbands
back

Memorial

In this park
the truer veterans'
memorial
lays on one of the
benches with his
arm over his head, dirty
wet socks on his feet, a
policeman
by his side
telling him to get a
move on

Entropy

Sometimes I feel
like I was made in the arms
of entropy, and every
part of me routes toward destruction, is
pulled in the direction of
chaos, going down the path
where it all breaks down
and I can search out
the rubble

Identity

You are always
connected
to the parts of yourself
you wish to escape from

The more you run
the further you'll be dragged
when you're brought back
to them

Dandelion Tattoo

She had
a dandelion tattoo
on her forearm
where the seedlings floated off
into birds

So beautiful that I
focused in
on the floating seeds
and the flying birds
and the pale raised lines
underneath
that had first marked her skin

Church

Observing church behavior in a
midwestern church – making note of the
over the top, the
smaller displays, the
gestures of devotions, the
church goers and songs and rhyme

And I can't help
but wonder

How much of this
is a genuine act
and how much of this
is an act
to convince others
while trying to convince
themselves

Scatter

As I tell my story, I
shatter myself and
scatter myself over
anyone who will listen,
and my soul intertwines and finds
a home parceled out
along the other scattered souls.

Forgiveness (Part 5)

What if forgiveness
is the one thing you still have
in the wreck of those who
wronged you – what if
handing over absolution means
handing over what little
power
remains?

Balance

…And there are still moments where I am struck with the imbalance of things – times when I gave too much and got too little and, in the end, learned too late that I had been played for a fool – times when the counterweight of growth and self-discovery and strength are not enough.

Those are the times I have to add weight to the words, "Never again," and pile them on – because I know only I can balance the scales for me. Wait on karma to do it and you'll be waiting a long time.

Platform

How easy it is
to love someone
when they are nothing
but a platform
for your own needs
and self-esteem

Anger

We are not
punished
for
our anger

We are punished
by
our anger

Small

I would become
so small
in your arms – and I liked that

I liked how tiny
I'd be

Until I realized how small
I had made myself
and how big
you decided to be

Heavy

You don't realize how
heavy your
secrets are
until you give them away
to trustworthy arms
and brazenly out
to the world at large

Nor do you realize how far
forward your shoulders had
slumped, until the weight is
gone,
and it's easy
to hold your head high again

Detest/Attest

"I can detest!" she says, and
in my mind, I correct her.
I can *attest*. But
then I wonder if it wasn't
so much of a mistake as it was
a slip – piping in her
confirmation as well as her
absolute disdain
for the subject at hand

Protection

I never sang as beautifully
as I did
the day
I realized you
did not deserve my silence

And I sang
the most beautiful song
the night
I realized you
were not worthy of my protection

Cut Through

She walks through the parking lot
deliberately in the path of cars, a look of
exasperation, entitlement,
frustration, as the cars approach, even as
they slow down for her

The wrinkles carved around her eyes and mouth
hinting
that the control over the cars is the only
reminder she has that she's not
been completely steamrolled
by the world

For a Fool

When played for a fool
the next step is not
to burn the castle down

But to step
boldly forward – and prove to the courts
your royalty, and the sheer folly
on their part,
for ever treating you that way

Full

How full I
became
when I decided
I couldn't live
on scraps

Pretense

She closes her eyes and
shakes her head when she says it, when she
says it's the
best thing
and she loves it so much

"Why does she
have to lie?" I think. "Why does she
have to pretend – to feel that
the only version of her that
can be accepted
is the role she plays
with her eyes closed?"

Reclaim

I reclaimed the city back, much like
I reclaimed my time, my energy
my heart

The same way I reclaimed the
music that made me think of you

By going over it all
over again
wearing out the notes and the streets

by going down
the well-worn roads a thousand new times
experiencing the world with new eyes and
new intentions, removing your name
where once it saturated

Until the roads, the scenes,
the time, my heart
and my life
are back to being mine

Broken Hearts Still Beat

It's a testament to
the human body – when we swore
we couldn't live without
someone, without them being
in our lives

And yet.

There's always a new dawn, a
next breath, because
broken hearts still beat, and
drained souls will replenish

When the Well Went Dry

When the well went dry
and all my understanding had been
used up

I was able to marvel
at the stone walls and the
depth of it all
before using the rocks of my
beloved well

To climb myself back out

Follow Up

When you find
yourself
saying,
"This will be
the death of me."

Follow it
with,
"And the
rebirth
of
a stronger me."

Bullet

It might feel
like life is shoving you
to the ground – but you'll eventually
look back and
realize
you were dodging a bullet
instead

Reaching Out

It is only in
the small hours of morning
do I feel the ache
to reach out
one last time

Only the early hours, when
I'm vulnerable and half-awake
and unaware of my surroundings

Which
in the end
is the perfect tableau
to the reality
of this dynamic

Phoenix (Part 2)

When a phoenix
rises from
the ashes
she leaves a trail of fire
smoldering through the sky
behind her

She does not
return
to the same flames
that incinerated her

Forgiveness (Part 6)

If you
forgive

Where can you
direct your attention, then,
if the pain returns?

He Asked If She Believed in God and Proceeded to Destroy Her Faith

He commended her
on her
spirit

and then did all the
things
that would inevitably
crush it

Faith

She had been so
brutally off in
knowing what was a line,
what was a lie, and
what was a genuine
truth

That more than
her lost trust
in him
she lost full faith
in herself
and her judgment

Burned

A tender soul with skin
charred from getting burned
will make both sword
and shield
from the scar tissues
and go forth blazing
with the most unquenchable
of fires

Catcall

He catcalls out, ignoring
my focused face, my
angry pace, the tight grip
on my purse

Apparently
an ass in leggings speaks
in louder tones than anything
else

Everything about my body
language screams,
"Don't fuck with me." Apparently
he only heard
half those words

When I Call

When I call
my mother talks in
half hour stretches, all
one sentence, a song of countless
"And"s "because"s and "but"s
where the only thing
connecting one thought
to the other
is her chorus of conjunctions

She speaks rapidly, as if
to be faster than her words, as if
she's on a runaway train and she's
hoping to jump off before it derails

She tries to bid goodbye four or five or
six times, only to get sidetracked and
frustrated at her straying

Like she's trapped in the car
and zooming past her junction
watching the scenery zip by
in a blurred and dizzying mess

Understand

There are just some things
That I don't understand

And some things I wouldn't want to if
Given the chance

Turbulence

There's a turbulence about him
that would do well to
find counter winds
to calm it down, to sooth the
hurricane, and, for once,
allow the homes to rest
without being battered against,
allow the boats to float without
fear of capsizing

But he'd rather spend that
energy
showcasing and
attempting to prove
he is the blue skies and
sunshine
that he wishes to be

Nostalgic

I'm not sure who I must pay
for passage on this trip
down memory lane – but the smell of
campfires at dusk has a way
of transporting down the expressway, directly
to all that was vibrant and
good as a kid – the cinders and smoke
a reminder
I'm the spirit I am because of this and not
despite it

God

It hurts my heart
to think that they
cannot fathom the idea
that God speaks in
math, and speaks in
science — in astrophysics, and
molecular biology. That God speaks
in theorems, not just theories.

But instead they believe God only speaks
in one language, one language only
that the song they get from God has
only one note, and they'll devote their lives
drowning out
the rest of the melody

Fearing Silence

I think some
fear the silence, because
without the noise, life can
saunter up and
whisper in their ear:

"Liar."

Forgiveness (Part 7)

Forgiveness and
rage cannot live in the
heart at the same time – but
forgiveness is not the
extinguisher to the fire, it will not
exile the rage and invade
the space and proclaim
victory

Forgiveness is not
the solution the hallmark cards
claim it to be

Phoenix (Part 3)

When you feel like
you've been
burned to ashes
you have two options:

1. Scatter the ashes
to the wind

2. Rise from them
like the Phoenix

Fix You

You are
broken in
the most fascinating
way

But I won't break
myself
just to figure out
why all the nuts and bolts
rattle like they do

I certainly won't
break myself
in an effort to fix you

Red Flags

Don't beat yourself up
for not seeing the red flags – nor
should you let it
turn every fabric in the breeze
into one

Let it be a chance to
hone in and fine tune
and become ready to transform
into a matador
should it ever happen
again

Bootstraps

We cling so tightly
to those damn
bootstraps

That we neglect to see
we're not
pulling ourselves up, so much as
dragging ourselves
(and each other)
down

Melancholy

I don't know
what to make of you,
with your subtle pings
whose origins I can't pin down

You are a strange and unknown
and yet polite house guest, never
clanging around
or slamming doors.

You are content with the back of the room,
just sitting there, letting your
presence be known simply by
letting out a sigh.

You won't tell me where you came from,
and you won't tell me how long you'll stay

And I don't know what to say, to tell you
you've overstayed your welcome
when you have proved to be nothing more
than another thing to take up space
in this home

Hurricane

I spoke so many words
to the empty air
in front of me

imagining you were here in its
place to
hear them

Instead

the vacuum of its absence swirled
in the gap between what I
needed and
what I had

Creating a
hurricane, letting me know
just how much this desire could destroy

Flawed

What flawed creatures we are

shattered souls desperately seeking out
the one thing we're unequipped to handle

Block

Two houses on
this city block
are burned – the insides
charred and just
the frames remain

It's almost like
even the buildings
are begging
for it all to be
demolished
and rebuilt
into something new

Build Something Beautiful

I am not a kind,
at ease person
when I'm hurt

The side of me comes out
in defense of a betrayed
heart or shattered
soul – and is not satisfied
by any salve of
revenge

She is only appeased when
I swear
to make something beautiful
from the pain
to build myself and
what's around me up
instead of tearing something
down

When I chose
to make
something beautiful
out of it

Freedom

The first step to
freedom is to learn
exactly
how the chains interlock
and exactly how small
the cage has been

Forgiveness (Part 8)

I don't forgive so much as I
observe the scales and wait
until I feel they have been
balanced again

I don't forgive so much as I
burn out the anger and rage
and venom – creating a bonfire and
inviting all my friends until it eventually
turns to ash and a new day dawns
and I walk away with nothing but
smoke behind me

I don't forgive so much as I
forget to hold a grudge, as time
wears on and I put enough things on
my plate that the misdeeds and
pain have rolled off the table
and I forget to hold its spot
by my place

I don't forgive so much as I
forget: forget the sharp, stinging
blows – because while it's fresh in
my memory, so is my inability
to grant clemency

Apology (Part 1)

Trust me on this one, darling
there is such thing
as being both
too late and too
soon to apologize

It is in the in between, when
the pain has fermented
with time – but not
enough has passed to
create distance, a
connecting point
between the crime and
moving on

Apology (Part 2)

In the end
what use
would it be
to get an apology

Those are just words.

I learned a
long time ago
that your words mean
nothing.

Ego

Of the many
things
I vow
to never do
again

I refuse
to feed
someone else's
ego – while I starve
alone.

Redoing

I once said you'd be
my beautiful undoing

little did I know I was
unraveling until all the
wrong stitches were out
and I had a chance
to start over

In a sense
I rebuilt anew
out of your destruction

Coping Mechanisms

And as I watched her at
yet another funeral, for
yet another member
of the family, as I watched her pick
a fight with yet another
living relative, that's when I
realized

This was a woman who was
never taught to cry, never
allowed to bare her heart, only
beat her chest and
bare her teeth, this was a woman
who was taught to face grief
by turning away and finding
someone to blame, someone
to point fingers
at, that
closed, clenched fists would stop her hands
from shaking

Demons (Part 1)

Until
you can
confront
your demons, you'll continue
to attract those
who only
confirm them

Explain Away

All the things
we accept
and
explain away

lay the foundation
for heavy and
unshakeable
regret

Mirror

She loved him the way
we do all things
that mirror our broken
past

Feverishly, and desperately
hoping that
this time the ending
will be different

Reborn

This is how I became
myself, through
fire and pain
until I was scorched of the earth
and reborn anew

Toxic Marriage

They were just
two people
trying to carve
the life they
wanted
out of the other
leaving gaping holes
and wounds and
knife marks, never getting
it was something meant to be
shared
between two people who
wanted
the same things

Anxiety-Induced

I start waking at 5, 4,
three in the morning, my brain
already on the
run, and from my
exhaustion I can tell
it has been for a while, as if
it was my brain's own chatter that had
disturbed my sleep

It was as if something sat
by the side of the bed, impatiently waiting
until it couldn't take it any longer, before
tugging wildly at my arm,
alerting me to something
I shouldn't sleep through

Thinking, thinking,
thinking -- my brain
on fire before the world wakes up
desperate for me not to stay docile
desperate to get me in
on the action

Free

When I had nothing
left to give
I had nothing
left to lose

So I dropped it all
and finally
broke free

Venom (Part 2)

Venom fills
up the tank
way faster
and fuller

than the
acknowledgment
that you cared for them
way more than they ever
cared for you

When you've given
it all, and get
nothing in return,
hatred makes for a
decent substitute

What to Do

"If you had but an iota of
understanding of what
was actually good for you, you'd actually
know what to do."

But I'm not an accountant, a
spreadsheet, a set of ROIs
and cost-benefit analyses

I am driven forward by the soul
and intuition, and what sings
in my heart at inopportune times

Father Issues

Interesting,
that we have so much
venom
for all the women
with "daddy
issues" – but no venom
left over
for all the men
who failed as fathers

Just One Foot

Just one foot
in front of the other
again and again
until what isn't needed falls
away and the distance between
lets you breathe again

Used Books

I buy used books as a way
of taking in and
celebrating the worn, the used
the dog-eared pages from
a past life's use

Instead of carting around
this
pristine thing, constantly worried
always concerned
for when the first page will fray

Resolve

How freeing it was
when the boiling pot of anger
simmered into a distilled resolve

Forgiveness (Part 9)

And he said,
"Pray for the people
you can't forgive.

Even if
the prayer just goes,
'Dear God,
Please give that son of a bitch
exactly
what he deserves.'"

Healing

Oh, my hurting heart

Healing is not
a straight line

You will go in
circles
and scribble back

One of the Two

And
with that
I threw my hands up
and said,
"Give me closure
or
the strength to let go
but I'm officially asking
for one
of the two."

How to Love a Narcissist

How tough it is
to show compassion
to someone who treats
love
like a vulnerability to exploit

who sees open heart like
an easy target

who take in acts of
love like fuel for a
monstrous machine spouting
black smoke behind it as it
goes

How do you give love
to someone
who only sees love
as something to take?

In Time

It will ache
just a little bit less
each time

Until eventually
the mornings stop feeling
so heavy, and your heart
doesn't feel so raw, and you can
breathe without sighing it out, and you take
another step forward
without looking back

Boundaries

The hardest thing
I've ever had to
learn
was how to not confuse building
boundaries with
putting up walls

New Chapter

I was chasing a
new chapter in my life
until I realized what I was
after was not a new chapter, but
a clean break
from my past

And I already knew such
a thing could never
happen

Try to run from your past
and it will take a
shortcut
to catch up with you

Good Nature

The hardest
hurdle when one's
good nature has been
abused and one must
set a boundary
(or more)

is accepting someone
abused their good
nature in the first place,
that someone saw their gentle ways
as something prime
for exploiting

Pain

Pain is not
weakness
leaving the body

Pain
is the body
attempting
to be stronger
than its environment

Freedom in Confession

The beauty
of owning up
to and atoning
for your sins
is that you get to move past them

instead of
having them
hang
over your head
like the sword of Damocles
wondering when
the thread
will break

The Truth About Letting Go

Here's the thing about letting go that
they don't tell you: they don't tell you
that it almost never happens as part
of a grand event – the reality is
you'll let go of control, only to grab the
reigns at the eleventh hour – and you'll
let go again, and then
go back on your word

They don't tell you that
letting go is non-linear.

That you will fall back
on your promises, you will
go in circles – but eventually
the compulsion gets a little
less compelling.

That you will go a little bit longer before
you break your promise to yourself.

You'll eventually hold on to
those reigns just a little less tightly.

And then, eventually, you find yourself
walking forward – and you'll not so much let go as
you'll
adapt – and you will have
relaxed your grip on it long before you're even aware
that, at some point,
you did, in fact, let it fall behind you

The Uses for an Apology from a Pathological Liar

You can take the words
and pick them apart – and then
rearrange them in a pretty
row, before
finding a chain and clasp and
creating a charming little
necklace with
what you've just made

Well, I mean, why not?

If they can string words together
for no other reason than because
it's shiny and cute and designed
to falsely charm or
placate the recipient
then why can't you?

Or maybe, you make a tower out of them, one that
you
build up and knock down, over and over, or maybe
you use them like noisy wallpaper, to
surround you and
assault your senses, or maybe
in an ironic twist
you create a doormat out of them
something now for you step on and
walk all over

Or maybe you make a big display of
walking out to the dumpster, and heaving over
everything they said – both the apology and

what came before – and point out all the garbage
within your periphery, both in front of you and
remembered
as a reminder of what you think of them

or

Maybe you do nothing
because the words have no face value
and you'll tire yourself out
trying to make them
worthwhile

Romance

She lost all interest
in being swept off her feet
once she realized it
usually meant
that the rug had been pulled
out
from under her

Special

Apparently, she'd rather
burn it all down
than admit
that she just wasn't special

Freeing

"Isn't it freeing," she said, "To know
that you
weren't special?"

Freeing, yes, the same way
an earthquake frees the land
of its buildings, a fire
frees the forest of
its trees, an
eviction notice frees
the tenants of
their lot

The understanding that
I wasn't special – I was just
the one dumb enough
to believe the lines
were genuine.

Unraveled

How quickly it all
unraveled
when I looked down
at
my clenched fist
and said,
"I know
there's still
hurt
in my heart."

Vengeance

In the end
her taste for vengeance was
actually
a hunger pain
for things to be balanced
again

Survival Mode

You can't live in survival mode – you just can't

It eventually burns away the edges of your
humanity, bulldozing the nuances
and intricacies in the name of
self-protection and
preservation.

It will take the very aspects, the very ways
and avenues that could
save your soul, and say, "Not now.
Not ever. I'm far too busy
trying to make it through – trying to
make it out alive."

This Is How You Get Through It

You get through it only
by accepting that
there is no such thing
as letting go – only
diving in and blazing through, only
going deep and forging on – and emerging out
on the other side
with the hope that you've now
left it all behind

Master Plan

How fascinating
to believe
that everything happens
for a reason

And yet

Be unable to
forgive
those for their past
actions, even though
you believe they were
destined to do them
and that it's all part
of a master plan

Promises

He constructed
lofty towers
with his promises
but without any
foundation they
crumbled, leaving
innocent civilians
to sort through the rubble
and search for loved ones
in the debris

Gambit

How it all changed when I learned
more from the other side – when her
words no longer sounded like blind
and naïve hope, but instead a gambit,
a dare for him to prove her wrong, a
subtle dig, a subverted declaration
that she's known who he actually is
all along

Joy

He spent so long stealing
fleeting moments of
happiness, that he
robbed himself
a chance at joy

Life Choices

There comes a point in life when the
weight of all your bad decisions comes
crashing down at once, and you
wonder if it's even possible
to dig yourself out from all the
rubble.

No wonder people just make their
homes in it instead.

Rot

He let his soul
rot
in the ground
because it was easier than
owning up to the mistakes of
the past, and unearthing the dirt
to make way for something new

Mistake

Perhaps my
biggest mistake when
I was lost
was turning to
anybody else
to find me

Recovery

You
survived
the catastrophe

You will
survive
the recovery

Divine Strength

Sweet child,
all your worst fears
were realized, and yet
you lived through it, lived
to tell the tale,
now with drier eyes and
a steady voice

How can you not see that
as a superpower, as proof
of your divine strength?

Guarded Gates

I was so scared
releasing the venom and
anger would
leave the gates open
for more pain to
come in

But keeping such
feelings contained
was destroying the very land
I thought I could protect

Blizzard

It was almost like
tragedy
was a blizzard – an
obliterating spectacle that
changed the world
around them in surreal and
drastic ways, but the real
ugliness came the day
after, when the sludge and salt and
dirt would remind
everyone
that life went on

Resentment, Returning

I do not
resent
the weights
that tore my muscles
down, so they'd repair
and grow back stronger

Same for the people
who did the same
to me

But

Unlike the weights
I won't be returning
to them
for a repeat
exercise

Forgiveness (Part 10)

I can
let go
of hurt
without
picking up
someone else's
redemption

Bear Witness

If I really am
the universe observing
itself, then
by God
I will bear witness
to as much
as I can
until the aperture
closes

Demons (Part 2)

You can't run
from your demons

They'll just find out
your destination
and meet you there

Demons (Part 3)

Never die
before
your demons do, lest
they follow you
into the afterlife

Trustworthy Love

Her "I love you"s were always
forced – as if
they were items to be dug up and
dragged out, heavy and clumsy and
presented feebly with tired
arms

My heart hurts to think
she never found herself
in trustworthy hands, never found a space
where the words could just tumble
from her mouth,
a place where love flows
fast, allowed to
cascade
from one heart to another

Spirit

What they don't tell you is that
you'll have to fight, every day
for your life – and if you're lucky, the fight
will revolve around keeping
your spirit alive, against
the crushing and
daily
grind

This world will go after
your spirit long after the fight
for food and shelter are won

When you are not fighting for your life, you will
fight
to keep the fire of living it lit

Becoming

I wondered:
why must we suffer, why must
we go through such dire
straits in order
to become ourselves

Because

It is only in
the bowels of hell
can we be introduced to our demons

And only through purgatory
do we have the means
of defeating them

Alpha

A true alpha wolf is never
by comparison strong.

A true alpha wolf would never
need to weaken the pack until
his rise to the top comes like
a technicality

But, in the end
it's too tempting for
some – for it's
easy to feel like
the wolf in charge
when you surround yourself
with half-starved pups

And the worst
is that
alpha wolves
have been
disproved

There is no
such thing – just loving
parents whose children
follow, packs made
from respect and trust

Princess

You cannot fathom
the mayhem that will be
unleashed
once the princess
figures out
she's a dragon

Return

I wonder how often I will
come back to this

like a neglected puppy, tossed
to the wilderness, but still
finding its way back to the place
it has mistakenly called home

What will I find – what
am I hoping to find?
Will one more return shed light
at a different angle, will the
sun strike down a different way,
will I step forward onto
the territory and realize
I can no longer stand the sight?

Am I hoping to return
to nothing? Am I hoping to
step forward and see the barren
wasteland when once there was
so much to take up space in
my mind? Am I hoping the
winds of karma have knocked
all the buildings down?

I wonder if there will ever
come a time when the siren's song
falls flat, and I'm not tempted
to dash myself upon the rocks,
even if it's under the guise of
seeing

if the cliffs have fallen into
the sea yet

But instead, I venture on, like
a puppy abandoned but taken in
by a pack of wolves, learning
how to growl and hunt and bite
and see any returning owners
with wild, feral eyes

Fangs

I'm still learning, still
checking myself when I
bare my fangs
when the proper
response is
to put salve on
a wound that's still not
healed

Rain

With the rain came the
scent of the ocean, the sweet
reminder of home, and
homecoming. The salty
sad reminder of my place
by the sea. A smell I get
100 miles in, landlocked
and alone.

Scars / Stars

I've wondered who is more
destructive – those who chase
stars or those who chase scars

Those reaching for the light or
those proving the darkness within.

I am to believe
the latter

For the first will eventually
find ground – the pull of
gravity saving the Icarus in all of us
but the other can be fueled by
a lifetime of tragedies
enough to get you
to the moon and back

Wasted

They say
no love
is ever wasted

But I sure did waste
my time, my energy, my
sense of better
judgment

And
certainly
I wasted

My peace of mind

Saving

I nearly
destroyed myself
in trying to save you
from yourself

Clearly
you were the wrong person
I needed to save

Retrospect

The intensity of the
retrospection has painted the
present day
in an unreal light.

But that's what you have to
do – when you want real change, you
return to the source and you
dive in headfirst and you
don't come back up for air until
you've shone light along the entire
submerged floor

Being Seen

Quantum physics
suggests
that the simple act of
observation
changes the object

Perhaps that's why we're all
so desperate to be seen
for perhaps in that
witnessing
there'll be hope of
transformation

That in their gaze
we'll become something new

Reconciling

Is life nothing
more than

reconciling

what we had been promised

with

what we have been given?

Renewal

Oh, the
sweet smell of spring
in the morning, and with it
the gentle hope
of renewal

Reprograming

Isn't that what we're doing, as we
become a little more self-aware and
self-actualized?

We become just a little more
informed
so we can retroactively
rewrite those messages?

So that we can read between
the lines and
decipher between
intent and outcome? That we stop
shooting the messenger so much as we
start to learn to
understand them?

That we stop fighting our
demons so much as we
learn to dance with them?

So Much

There was once
so much
I wanted to say to you

Then

So much
I wanted to say
about you

And now

So many other
soul-filling
life-fulfilling
topics, to talk about,
so many other areas to enjoy
so many other aspects
to explore
that don't involve
you

Find Your Own Fortune

Be care
not to go
bankrupt
trying to settle
unfinished
business

Wordplay

The phrase
"mad as
hell"
is a nice
reminder
that these
emotions
will only drag
you down
into the flames

Even for God

If nothing
else
perhaps
Christianity
can remind me
that brimstone
and vengeance
is Old
Testament
even
for
God

Gates

The greatest freedom
came
not when I burst through
the gates, but when
I stopped caring
that he locked me in
them
in the first place

Float

Perhaps the
scariest thing
I had to do in the
wake of it all
was to remember how to
write to explore oceans again
instead of just
to keep my head above
water

Image

I've wished you many
different, contradictory things
over the years – but now
I think
I just wish you the
bravery
to stand square in front of the
mirror
and stare
without trying to paint
a new image over it

Forgiveness (Part 11)

They say time
heals all wounds, but
I have to disagree

We wouldn't have to dig
into childhood traumas if time
really was the salve
it markets itself to be.

But time gives
distance.

Enough space between
you and the event that you
have a chance to address and
dress your wounds – that you're
far enough away that the
person who hurt you can't
rip the bandage off, exposing your
rawness to the open air

And perhaps that's what forgiveness
must look like
sometimes: to wait until
distance has blurred both the pain and the
person who wronged you, until the sharp edges
lose focus – so far removed you simply
do not care if words of forgiveness
tumble from your mouth like a
muttered afterthought – and you care even less
if the words ever reach the
recipient's ear

How It Started

When I met you, my heart didn't
shout from the mountaintops
blaring depthless vows and singing
love songs and spouting
declarations, promises, deafening tones

My body didn't yell out
like a castaway at sea to the lifeboat
in front of me, screaming
to be saved, calling out over
the tides and currents until
my voice went hoarse

My spirit didn't fill the room with
ear-piercing bellows, the sounds echoing off
walls and making windows shake

There were no loud and sweeping moments, no
grand gestures or scenes, nothing that could
cause an avalanche or shatter glass

My soul simply saw yours and went, "Oh.
There you are.

I think I've been looking for you
for all of my life."

A gentle sentence, whispered
like a breeze through the leaves

And my head's been pounding and
my ears have been ringing
ever since

Spring

How fitting it is
to wash the salt from
my shoes, in the
puddles of a new
spring day

Dido

Perhaps mine
is like the story
of Dido, who
let her kingdom
crumble in the face
of ill-begotten love, but
instead of driving
a sword through her
chest, she returned
to build her empire
and make up for
lost time

Delicate Dance (Pt 1)

This delicate
dance
we do, touching
the word "love"
with our toes, letting it
graze past our knuckles, breathe
gently on our skin, whisper
as it moves

Trying it on
for size, letting our
mouths, our
tongues taste it, seeing
how it feels as it
describes everything else
around us

This beautiful little
dance, scooping up
Love and letting it
trickle off our palms, watching
just how close to the
line we'll go, seeing
how many times more I can
say,
"You're
amazing," when what I
really mean is,
"I love you."

Peace at War

I've learned
to make peace
with the fact
that
certain things
I might never
make peace with

Confronting

Funny
how once I stopped
fearing
what the answers would
be
when I stopped clawing
the walls
for an immediate
solution

that I learned how deep
this could get, how
full I could feel, and how
beautiful it is
from this point of view

Sodden

Oh, beautiful one
if you only
knew

the universe is sodden
with words I want to say to you

Good Intentions

You could feel
her good heart
trying to shine through
but everything
inside was so
broken and
shattered
that the light reflected off
jagged and
scattered

Venom (Part 3)

I feel like the snake
who had the cloth-covered cup forced
upon her – who was thrust
into circumstance where
she had no choice but to strike

and pump her venom
viciously
into what she thought
was the enemy

only to realize that the universe
was making
an antidote for the
poison within her

Sum

You are more
than the sum of
your tragedies

Just the same, you are
more
than the sum of
your victories over
them

Details

I want to
delicately dance with the
details and savor the
moments that play
like snippets in
the back of my mind and
I want to hold these
memories with both
hands and
bring them close to my face
and feel their lingering
heat

Unknown

I walked into
the room, and the
smell
brought me back to
a place – and the memory
was enough to
make me want to weep

The only thing
was I couldn't remember
with words or sight
what this place was

It was a private conversation
between my nose and
my brain
whispers that I got fragments of
in a thrumming heart and
filling eyes

How crazy
to be brought so powerfully back
to a spot
where you're blind – to a place
where you cannot touch
or hear, but still feel yourself there
entirely

After Reconnecting with a Part of Your Soul

The world is a little brighter
in its wake, the lines are sharper, the
colors vibrant, the subtle sounds echoing
like symphonies

The resonance of the world is
a little deeper, the echoes of
the connection lingering
in every breath, every heartbeat,
every heavy truth, every
bold and beautiful reality

Siren

She sang the most
beautiful song she knew
from her kitchen – as
she cleaned dinner plates and
saucepans; sang a melody that
made her soul ache, sang with
all her heart – sang the way
her husband would once
coax her to sing
when they were
younger, to sing
with less trepidation and more
soul

She imagined her husband
watching her, listening to
her from his spot
in the living room, hearing her
sing her notes, the rise and
fall, the verse, the chorus, the
bridge

She imagined captivating him
like she did when they were
young – becoming the siren and
winning him over, winning him
back, so that
he'd look at her with both new
and old eyes, so that what
had been dropped and lost
would be found again in
her notes echoing off

the walls

She heard her husband
pipe in as the song
hit its refrain.

"I'm trying to watch
the game – could you please
keep it down?"

She finished the dishes in silence.

Making Space

It's a subtle but
distinct
difference

Holding space for
someone
to be in your life
and chasing after them
to spend time
with you

Annual / Perennial

There are two types of love, like
flowers at the store – the
perennials, the year-round, the
ones meant to withstand the winters and
bloom again

And the annuals, meant
to bloom beautiful, but also
destined to die when the
first frost hits

Is there any bigger tragedy
than to confuse the perennial for
the annual, or
force the temporary love into
forever?

In Love

In love,
I will remember
to be a mirror
and not
a spotlight

The Worst Thing

The worst thing we
can do when
battling our demons, our
self-loathing, is to carry
on and pretend
like we've liked ourselves
all along

Mending

Perhaps it was not
the fact that her
husband had passed, or that
she had spent the last forty years
in a quiet type of
misery, standing by as he
never learned
to conquer his
demons

But the fact that, at no
point, did the wounds and
cracks from her
own past be tended
to, her own breaks not
even attempted a
mend, a shattered spirit destined to
go
to her own grave
in pieces

Sisterly

She caps off the night
the way she caps off every
night on a family
event: declaring the
we don't
hang out enough, that
we need
to do more
family things, that she
misses me

But after turned down invitations and
conversations that went
nowhere, I know I'm to
smile and nod and head
out (these
proclamations always
as we're saying
good-bye)

It's almost like she knows
no other way to
bond outside of false
promises and
empty claims

Like the man who raised us
never showed us
how to love
with genuine acts
instead of
words to be slurred
out at parties
with one foot out
the door

Long Term Love

Perhaps it's no longer the type
of love that stops the
breath and overloads
the heart, perhaps
she won't tear herself
to shreds in his
absence – perhaps
it's no longer the loud, ringing
romance, the kind that
deafens the ears
to all outside
sounds

But it's the love of a warm
sunny morning, one that
fills the heart, the love that
you can melt into like a tight
embrace, a love that builds her
up in his presence, the kind
of love that plays
the loveliest song
if only she can stay still enough
to listen

Time

Sometimes I can see
the pieces of time laid out
before me, coming together
like a puzzle, ever part
in its destined spot, coming together
to make the image whole

Sins

I've had enough
paying for
sins I
already atoned for
just because someone
else refuses
to atone for theirs

Unapologetic

I've done enough
apologizing
when I should've been shouting

So I will live my life
unapologetically
and shout louder than the resistance

Eggshells

How little
I cared
about the eggshells around me
once I finally
learned
to put my foot down

Confrontation

Wounds
left
to fester
will do
exactly that

Villain

Sweet child
congratulations
you got the villain you
wanted to make this
all black and
white

but do not let it
cover over
not just
the shades of gray, but
all the colors that have
been there
the entire time

Clearing Away

You are worth so
much more than
treating parts of your life like
unwanted items in the fridge

leaving them to rot, letting them
affect the things around it
before you finally find
reason to clear it
away

you are worth more than mold and
disgust

Justice

I watched
the car
speed down the
shoulder on the
left side, blazing
past
all of us stuck
in lawful, traffic-jammed
lanes

Just speeding past, no
trooper to pull him over, no
officer to run his
plates – just
illegal travel until
the shoulder narrowed and
he slipped right back
in the leftmost
lane

And I found myself
fuming
at the car that let
him in, at the
lack of consequences,
that someone could
pull something like that
off,
and then just slip back
into everyday life
like nothing had
happened

Break Free

He said,
"If you're going to
heal, if you're going to
break free, you have
to embrace the
nuance.

Even caricatures are
full sketches of
people – just with
exaggerated parts
about them."

What She Wants

Perhaps
it's for the best
that she doesn't know
what she wants

The world will burn
when she finally
figures it out

Salt

More word play:

how quickly the tone
shifts when you subtract
a few words, when

"the salt of the earth"
means practically the
opposite
of
"salt the earth"

Like all it takes for a
gem to destroy all
that is valuable
is to take away something
small but
vital

Drive

Gone are the days
when I would let
others grab
the steering wheel from
my hands (or, worse,

when I wouldn't
hold the reigns at all, allowing
just about anyone to pick them
up)

and resign myself
to the passenger seat,
praying that they'll go
in the direction I was heading,
that they'll make the turns I
wanted to take, and cursing
the streets, as I pass them
by on the wrong path, one that I
never chose

Big Girl Pants

If I had known
how good
the big girl pants
feel
how right of a
fit
they are,
I would've put them on
a long time ago

Pick One

Spend your life:

- uncovering and
discovering

or

- denying who you are

Pick one.

Making Waves

Refusing
to make waves
eventually
tips your own boat
over

Humble

She was a kind
and humble person
so long as she was allowed
to be the best

and his spirit is
magnanimous
so long as he feels
no one's been given
more than what
he's got

What To Do After The Thrill Is Gone

After the fiery flames of passion stop
screaming, "Yes!" – as if in the throes
of ecstasy, listen
for the rumblings of the soul
as it repeats its
vital reply, its deep and
baritone and constant chant:
Yes.
Yes.
Yes.

The Past

Yes, the past – aren't you quite
the mirror? But a peculiar kind: the type
that reflects back how
different things are, or points out
the origin of things. Its
reflection is a measurement
of how far you've come

Reaching In

It is in the
warming hours of
the morning, when I crawl
back into your
side of the bed, nestled
in the small space between
you and the edge,
nestled in
the crook of your arm

As the world wakes up, the morning
giving way
to the day, when I'm
out of my dream world but choosing
to stay in this divine
space

Which
in the end
is the perfect tableau
for this wonderful
little thing

Shed

Sometimes I'll shed
the coat of
"I should want this," and
instead embrace
the naked understanding
that I don't want what
I've been told to want, that I won't be
what others around me have
become

Burn

I burned brightly that night

and with it
everything
that should've been left
to dust
went up in smoke

Light Up

She'd let her whole life
burn if it meant that
the night sky would light up
like it never had before

A Pause in Poetry

I realized I hadn't
written much poetry as
of late

Perhaps
I should consider
it a blessing, to be
in a state
where the things
in my heart don't
spill out
in jagged lines
and incomplete phrases

Shards

I write the way
one might smash a fist
into a mirror, and then
turn it towards the world: in
hopes that perhaps
one or more of those
shards will reflect something
back
for those who take the
time to look (even if
my fist is bloodied in
the meanwhile)

And perhaps I'm also
hoping
people will see the
cuts on my
hand and realize
that it looks
way worse
than it actually feels

Fording Across

Just outside
the echo chamber
of
"boys will be boys"
stands a chorus of
strong women, and
those that support
them, singing loud
and in defiance
demanding their song
be heard

Onwards

We might be fucked.

We might be barreling down the
darkest, saddest, most heartbreaking
dead end road, guardrails up to cause
a crash if we veer away

We may be without hope.

But we get moments like these, moments that
fill the soul and prop us up, and I'll be damned
if I won't fight for that, and see this
to its bloody end

Inventory

Those
who refuse to
take inventory
of their demons
will have
no idea
how big the army will be
when they attack

Intimacy

In the space
between
closed off gates and
pillaged lands
you will find me
navigating
the soil, figuring
my way, determined
never to return
to either extreme

Boundaries (Part 2)

Remember:
Forgiving debts
doesn't mean
they get to take
another loan out
from you

Accommodate

How many times I wish
I had just said, "No, we
are not on the same
page – I've just been
jumping from my book
to yours."

Like a Love Song

I loved you
like a love song — in that
it was full of melody
and words that
fit the beat, but ultimately
meant to end
as the final note
played

Drowning

And that's when
I had no choice but
to look her in the eye
and say, "You have
a lot to figure
out – but I'm getting
dragged
through the current
as you navigate
those
waters
and it's time
to cut the cord
before I drown."

Letting Go

Like a constant nudge from
the universe — "the amazing things that
will come once you
genuinely let go"

— and then I did,
and then it did.

Unfolding

How beautiful
life's potential become
when it stopped being about
mirrors so much as it became
about unfolding

Bloom

The things that she
could blossom into
if she were just
given
enough garden space

Golden Days

There are golden days
when life feels like something
that can be sipped from
the finest cup, when the
intangible
dances around my hands, through
my fingers – when the
very spirit of
what drives us forward
makes itself a humble guest
in my skin

These are the moments when
I savor the flavor, the touch, the texture, the
taste – find some way to store it
for later, for when the cup feels hollow
and the dance floor has been
vacated

Precious Gem

What a precious gem, when
a kiss on the forehead feels
like a gasp in the dark feels like
a tracing caress feels like
a shared smile as
the words pour out

An Infinite Thing

The heart is an
infinite thing,
and yet still there's a
piece of it that is yours
and yours alone

Delicate Dance (Pt 2)

I've learned
to appreciate
this delicate dance
instead of worrying
about when the music will

stop

or if my partner is going
to step on my toes

Gentle Thanks

In the gentle
silence, I can hear
the soft
whispers of all the
things
that nourish my soul

Salvation / Denial

I'd rather stumble
through briars on the
path to salvation

Than deliberately plunk
down in the middle of
the forest and pretend my
branch-made lean-to
is actually a mansion

Forgiveness (Part 12)

Perhaps
for me
forgiveness is what's
left
after all the venom
and righteous
indignation has been
burned out – when
nothing remains but the
ash and residue
and the only thing one
can do
is set it to the wind

Forgiveness (Epilogue)

And just like that
instead of trying
to find
forgiveness, she found
it came to her – only when
she was ready to
look, only when
giving it away did not feel
like losing once again

About the Author.

Abby Rosmarin is the author of the Amazon bestseller *In the Event the Flower Girl Explodes*, as well as *No One Reads Poetry, Chick Lit & Other Formulas for Life*, and *I'm Just Here for the Free Scrutiny*. Her work has featured in *The Huffington Post, Bangalore Review, Storgy Magazine, Esthetic Apostle, Thought Catalog* and others. Abby is a retired commercial model and registered yoga teacher. She currently lives in New Hampshire with her husband.